Religious or Spiritual:

How the Difference Can Affect Your Happiness

Also By Lee and Steven Hager

The Beginning of Fearlessness: Quantum Prodigal Son

The Gospel of Thomas: Where Science Meets Spirituality

Lee and Steven Hager

Religious or Spiritual:

How the Difference Can Affect Your Happiness

Oroborus Books

Religious or Spiritual: How the Difference
Can Affect You Happiness

Copyright © 2011 by Lee and Steven Hager

Published by Oroborus Books

The Beginning of Fearlessness/Oroborus Books
website and blog:

http://www.thebeginningoffearlessness.com

ISBN 10: 0978526155
ISBN 13: 978-0-9785261-5-3
LCCN: 2011936755

This book is dedicated to those who have the courage to listen to thier heart and follow its wisdom.

The teacher who is wise does not bid you to enter the house of his wisdom, but rather leads you to the threshold of your mind. —Khalil Gibran

The world as we have created it is a process of our thinking. It cannot be changed without changing our thinking.
—Albert Einstein

Only words and conventions can isolate us from the entirely indefinable something which is everything. —Alan Watts

I do not believe the same God who has endowed us with sense, reason and intellect has intended us to forgo their use.
—Galileo

Contents

Religious or Spiritual:

How the Difference Can Affect Your Happiness

Part One:
Spiritual

Introduction

I am here to pull out the chair beneath your mind—and watch you fall upon God.

—Hafiz

Can the way you approach God affect your happiness? Does it really matter whether you're religious or spiritual? Is there any real difference between the two? Most of us assume the words 'religious' and 'spiritual' mean the same thing. And why not, since the two words are often used interchangeably. But that wasn't always the case. If you look up the original meanings of 'religious' and 'spiritual,' you'll find out they once described two very different approaches to the Divine. The further we dug into the subject, the more astonished we were. Finally, we realized that the loss of the original meanings of these words was affecting the happiness of millions of people around the globe. How did this change in understanding come about, and what does it mean for you?

Language

We're all constantly absorbing information, and much of it comes to us through written or spoken language. Language is extremely powerful. It can be used to spread valuable information, but it also has the ability to manipulate our thinking and change our world view without our awareness or our consent. Language is, without question, fluid and dynamic. Words are nothing more than temporary symbols that we use by unspoken agreement. This quality allows language to keep up with our changing world, but it's also where communication breaks down and word meanings are lost. Here are just a few of the reasons we all experience communication problems:

■ The same word means something slightly

different to each and every person that uses it because they're filtering it through their own experience. For example, if someone says the word apple, you might think of a fruit that's red, sweet and crispy and I might be thinking of a tart green fruit. But, the same word might cause someone else to think of a computer.

■ Words have different meanings in different locales.

■ Words take on different meanings within small groups.

■ Word meanings constantly evolve and devolve over time.

■ Words fade out of use on a regular basis because the thing they symbolized becomes obsolete. Have you ever heard the words 'himation,' 'pallium' or 'pourpoint?' They were common clothing items worn in ancient

Greece, Rome and mediaeval Europe, but the words faded out of use along with the clothing styles.

■ At times words remain in use, but the meanings change drastically (for example: neat, cool, bad, gay or chill). These changes usually happen very quickly. At other times a word continues to be used, but the meaning goes through a series of subtle changes that take place over a long period of time.

When the original meaning of a word is lost, it doesn't necessarily follow that it was no longer valuable. Meanings may change because perception, interest, values, knowledge or influence changes. And at times, a change in meaning is forced or manipulated. But change doesn't necessarily imply improvement. As we examine the original meanings of the words 'religious' and 'spiritual,' keep in mind that changes in language can be helpful, but also harmful. Since the word spiritual has undergone the most dramatic changes, we'll look at that first.

Chapter One

The important thing is this: to be able at any moment to sacrifice what we are for what we could become. —Charles Du Bois

Lost Meanings

In our world, spiritual can mean almost anything. Marketers often associate the word with beauty products, exercise classes, health food, a trip to the spa, or anything else that's supposed to relieve stress. Spiritual is used interchangeably with religion, or it can describe the more personal aspects of religion. You may also have heard it used to designate the difference between organized religion and 'new age' teachings. Sometimes it defines a private search for a connection with the Divine. This last description hits closer to the original meaning, but it still misses the original flavor of the word. Why should you care? As the meaning changed, a direct avenue of approach to the Divine was hidden.

It's fairly obvious that the word spiritual is built on the root word spirit, but the meaning of spirit may surprise you. Spirit comes from the Latin *spiritus*, which means "to breathe." Christians are often taught to associate spirit with "the breath of life." This connection was made in the creation story found in the Bible book of Genesis. At Genesis 2:7, we're told that after God made Adam out of dust, He "breathed into his nostrils the breath of life; and man became a living being." That sounds reasonable since we associate breathing with life, but there's far more to spirit than breath.

Like most religions, Genesis pictures God as a supernatural being that exists outside of creation. Spirit is described as a force that God uses to bring inanimate material objects to life by infusing them with breath. God also withdraws spirit/breath, and when that happens, the animate object becomes inanimate again. We've labeled these two states, breathing and not breathing, 'life' and 'death,' but is that an accurate description of what's happening? Is spirit something that's given and withheld at God's whim, or is it something more?

'Inside' and 'Outside' Gods

In the Genesis creation story, God made an inanimate material universe, used spirit to animate parts of it, and then supervised it from a distance. For convenience, we'll call this the 'outside' God. Most us have been taught to think of God this way, but *spiritus* originally described something far more intimate. *Spiritus* isn't something used by the Divine, it *is* the Divine. In the original meaning, the Divine was not thought of as a being that was separate from creation, but a life force that permeates, actuates and continually sustains everything in existence, both animate and inanimate. In this scenario, it would be impossible for

Ultimate Reality to exist outside creation, because everything that exists is made of the 'stuff' of the Divine and is continually sustained by it. To differentiate, we'll call this the 'inside' God.

Now we're faced with two very different pictures of God and spirit. Why is it important to understand the differences between these 'outside' and 'inside' Gods? A God that creates and operates the universe from outside can either be involved in creation or be indifferent to it. The issue of involvement constantly comes up for anyone who worships an 'outside' God. Not only do they wonder if God cares, they usually feel that they have to devise ways to try to attract and keep their God's interest. Since outside Gods appear to give and take life sustaining spirit at will, their worshipers feel their life depends on appeasing their 'outside' God. Most religions have decided that worship, obedience, ritual and sacrifice are needed to placate 'outside' Gods.

Outside Gods are also said to rule separate realms that exist beyond the material universe. These realms are dualistic in nature. In other words, they're usually extreme opposites, like heaven and hell. Most religions teach that outside Gods can extend your life by sending you to one of these realms after the death of the physical body. But this presents a problem. If the death of the physical body occurs when spirit/breath is withdrawn, how does one continue living after the body dies? Most religions teach that there's another spark of life called the soul, which exists within the body while it's animated, and leaves the body at death. Where this soul ends up usually depends on whether or not the body followed certain rules during life. But none of these problems exist when Ultimate Reality *is* the universe.

Since the 'inside' God *is* spirit that continually permeates and sustains everything in existence, several important factors become evident:

- Spirit isn't a tool or force to be used; it's not something that's given and taken away.

- Everything in existence, whether it appears to be animate or inanimate, is alive because it's part of Divine Spirit.

- Life can't end. Scientists tell us that matter can become energy, and energy can become matter, but the sum total never changes. What we think of as death is actually a transition between matter and energy.

- It would be impossible for the 'inside' God to be disinterested or uninvolved in creation since the Divine *is* creation.

(We realize this statement brings up many questions since a quick look at world conditions appears to testify to an uninterested or uncaring God. The "problem of evil" is addressed and thoroughly answered in our book *The Beginning of Fearlessness: Quantum Prodigal Son.*)

'Outside' gods, goddesses, angels, devils and demons have monopolized the world's religions, but individual spiritual seekers throughout the ages have recognized the 'inside' God. Although these seekers have usually been separated by time and distance, they each understood that *everything* exists 'in spirit' and literally *is* spirit.

Nearly 1,500 years before Jesus lived, ancient Indian sages living along the banks of the upper Ganges wrote about this 'inside' presence. Their collected poetic teachings are known as the *Upanishads*. Upanishad means "sitting down near" or "at the knee of," and pictures the way students sat by their teachers. But the word Upanishad also has a meaning that's significant in our understanding of the word spiritual. It means, "setting to rest ignorance by revealing the knowledge of the supreme spirit." In other words*, to leave ignorance behind, we must*

understand the all-pervading nature of spirit.
Let's look at a few excerpts from the Upanishads
and let them speak for themselves:

As by knowing one lump of clay, dear one,

We come to know all things made out of clay

That they differ only in name and form.

While the stuff of which all are made is clay;

So through that spiritual wisdom, dear one,

We come to know that all of life is one.

In the beginning was only Being,

One without second.

Out of himself he brought forth the cosmos

And entered into everything in it.

There is nothing that does not come from him.

Of everything he is the inmost Self.

He is the truth; he is the Self supreme.

You are that. . .you are that.

—Chandogya Upanishad

Sometimes this all-pervading life force is called "Divine Ground." The Aitareya Upanishad explains more clearly just what this Divine Ground is:

Before the world was created, the Self

Alone existed; nothing whatever stirred

Then the Self thought: "Let me create the world."

Who is this Self on whom we meditate?

It is the Self by which we see, hear, smell, and taste,

Through which we speak in words. Is Self the mind

By which we perceive, direct, understand,

Know, remember, think, will, desire, and love?

These are but servants of the Self, who is

Pure consciousness.

This Self is all in all.

He is all the gods, the five elements,

Earth, air, fire, water and space; all creatures.

Those who realize [Ultimate Reality] live in joy

And go beyond death. Indeed,

They go beyond death.

So far, you've learned that spirit is Divine, and the Divine is a life force that permeates and connects everything in existence. And, you've discovered, "You are that." But what is "that?" The *Aitareya Upanishad* tells us this Divine Ground is "pure consciousness." This may sound very odd if you've been taught that God is a supernatural being that's separate from creation and has qualities very similar to humans. But recent discoveries in the field of quantum physics support the Upanishad teachings.

Divine Ground

Scientists known as material realists believe that only matter exists. They feel certain consciousness evolved from matter and is no more than another form of matter. They believe that when your body dies, all your thoughts die with it. Since material realists believe consciousness evolved, they think matter that hasn't climbed far enough on the evolutionary ladder can't be conscious. Although these scientists have diligently tried to discover how matter produced consciousness, their attempts have failed.

On the other hand, physicists have discovered that consciousness permeates even the subatomic particles at the most fundamental levels of the universe. Since these particles are the foundation of all matter, we must conclude that all matter is conscious. However, that doesn't mean that everything in existence experiences the same level of awareness. You could think of consciousness as a light that's either off or on, and awareness as a rheostat that can be adjusted from dim to bright. This discovery also suggests that consciousness was present at the beginning of the universe and has never had to evolve.

If the material realists were right and consciousness evolved from matter, then our thoughts are individual and private. But Shankara, a sage who lived about 900 years after Jesus, explained that one shared consciousness permeates and unites everything in existence. In *The Crest-Jewel of Discrimination*, he said:

> *You are pure consciousness, the witness of all experiences. Your real nature is joy. . .[the Self] is pure consciousness. . .You are the [Self] the infinite Being, the pure unchanging consciousness, which*

*pervades everything. Your nature is bliss
and your glory is without stain.*

Physicists have discovered this shared consciousness at the foundation of the universe. Communication takes place between subatomic particles faster than the speed of light. Scientists have looked in vain for other explanations, but the phenomenon could only be explained by the presence of one shared consciousness. Physicist Erwin Schrödinger correctly observed, "Consciousness is a singular for which there is no plural." You've learned that spirit is the Divine, and the Divine is a life force *and* a shared field of higher consciousness that creates an impermeable bond between everything in existence. But what about the personal aspects of God?

Some Eastern teachings focus on spirit as a Divine Ground or matrix that connects, supports and sustains the universe, but has no personal aspects. In the West, we usually think of God in the opposite way, a human-like being that exists outside creation, but is personally accessible. People on both sides of the argument often insist that God must be either a force without a personality *or* be a personality that does not serve as a ground or matrix. But a Divine Ground and a personal God are not mutually exclusive. Many spiritual seekers have understood that Ultimate Reality is a life force or ground, but the quality of that force is love.

The writers of the Upanishads knew that "all life is one," but they also said that this life force is "The Lord of love and the source of peace and joy." The *Nasadiya Sukta*, a very ancient text that may have preceded the Upanishads, says, "In the beginning Love arose, which was the primal germ cell of the mind." In other words, spirit is a life force/Divine Ground, shared higher consciousness and love.

Valentinus, an early Christian gnostic, agreed that love was the reason Ultimate Reality became the universe:

Since the Father was creative, it seemed good to him to create and produce what was most beautiful and most perfect to himself. For he was all love and love is not love if there is nothing to be loved.

The Sufi sage, Rumi, made the same point when he said, "Without Love, nothing in the world would have life." He explained:

You are—we all are—the beloved of the Beloved, and in every moment, in every event of your life, the Beloved is whispering to you exactly what you need to hear and know. Who can ever explain this miracle? It simply is. Listen and you will discover it every passing moment. Listen, and your whole life will become a conversation in thought and act between you and Him, directly, wordlessly, now and always. It was to enjoy this conversation that you and I were created.

Chapter Two

The attitude of faith is to let go, and be-come open to truth, whatever it might turn out to be. —Alan Watts

What Spiritual Means

We've taken a lengthy detour, but we've discovered that spirit is Ultimate Reality. In turn, Ultimate Reality is a Divine energy field of life, shared consciousness and love. We exist within that field, 'in spirit.' Even Albert Einstein recognized the significance of this Divine Ground of consciousness when he said, "The field is the only reality." Since that's the case, what does spiritual mean?

Although we're all constantly 'in spirit,' it's a state few of us are aware of. When the word spiritual was originally used, it signified awareness of our true state, 'in spirit.' When we're aware, we know that we are an inseparable part of everything in existence, including the Divine. How do we reach that state of awareness?

Understanding oneness and shared consciousness on an intellectual level is a start, but awareness must ultimately be *experienced*, not talked about or studied. When you got your first bike, watching others may have given you some idea how to ride. And your parents may have tried to explain the necessity of balance and momentum, but you had to get on the bike and experience the sensation before you understood exactly what they were talking about. The same is true of spiritual awareness.

Shankara pointed out the difference between learning and experience when he said, "A clear vision of the Reality may be obtained only through our own eyes, when they have been opened by spiritual insight—never through the eyes of some other seer. . .Study of the scriptures is fruitless as long as [Ultimate

Reality] has not been experienced. And when [Ultimate Reality] has been experienced, it is useless to read the scriptures." (*The Crest Jewel of Discrimination*)

Most of us have been taught that we can learn about God by studying a holy book, listening to a church sermon or attending Bible classes. But spiritual masters have never been interested in learning *about* Divine Presence; they expect to 'know' the Divine as you would know a friend or lover. For them, it's not an intellectual pursuit; spirituality is a "do-it-yourself, first-hand experience."

What Gnosticism and Spirituality Have In Common

People who accumulate vast amounts of knowledge are often considered experts, but knowledge and 'knowing' are not the same thing. When you take in information, you always get it second-hand. When you 'know,' you experience it for yourself. This direct knowing is also called *gnosis*. Although gnosis has been a part of the mystical segment of most religions, including Christianity, it's not a religion. Gnosticism isn't really an 'ism.' It can't be organized, let alone institutionalized, because no one else can experience the Divine for you.

Gnosis is best understood as the direct experience of Spirit. It's a personal, intuitive process. The experience takes place when we connect with Ultimate Reality through higher consciousness. This may sound difficult at first, but remember that you're already part of the one shared consciousness of Ultimate Reality. People have been experiencing Ultimate Reality throughout history, and those who 'know,' agree on these points:

■ The world of matter is no more than a temporary manifestation of a life force that permeates the universe.

■ A change of consciousness is required to become aware of, and experience, that divine life force.

■ Everyone possesses the ability to experience the Divine.

■ Experiencing and uniting with Divine Presence is humanity's highest purpose.

In other words: Life-giving intelligence permeates everything in existence. That intelligence wants to be known and can be known. These principles are known as the perennial philosophy.

The Gnostic Jesus

You may be surprised to know that many of Jesus' earliest followers knew Jesus as a gnostic teacher. These followers wrote gospel accounts of Jesus' life and teachings that tell a very different story than the New Testament gospels. In the gnostic *Gospel of Thomas,* Jesus told his followers to stop looking outside themselves for answers because "Whoever has come to know the world has discovered a corpse." Instead, he said, "If you bring forth what is within you, what you have will save you." He added, "When you know yourselves, then you will be known, and you will understand that you are children of the living Father. But if you do not know yourselves, then you dwell in poverty, and you are poverty."

Although many of his followers were still interested in an 'outside' God, the gnostic Jesus knew his followers would find the Divine inside. In *The Book of Thomas the Contender,* Jesus reminded his followers that they are an inseparable part of the Divine. He taught them that when they understand this truth, they will finally understand Ultimate Reality, "For he who has not known himself has known nothing, but he who has known himself has at the same time already achieved knowledge about the depth of the All."

The gnostic Jesus knew that no one else can experience the Divine for us. When he told his disciples to "seek first the kingdom," he was not offering to do it for them. Instead, he told them, "The kingdom of God is not coming with your careful observation nor will people say, 'Here it is' or 'There it is,' because the kingdom of God is within you." (Luke 17:20-21)

In *The Dialogue of the Savior*, the Gnostic teacher Silvanus pointed out that the One Mind of consciousness we share with Ultimate Reality is the only teacher we need:

> *Bring in your guide and your teacher. The mind is the guide. . .Live according to your mind. . .Acquire strength, for the mind is strong. . . Enlighten your mind. . .Light the lamp within you."*

Silvanus went on to explain that no one can experience the One Mind of shared consciousness for us. Each of us must take personal responsibility and access the One Mind experientially:

*Knock on **yourself** as upon a door and walk upon **yourself** as on a straight road. For if **you** walk on the road, it is impossible for **you** to go astray. . .Open the door for **yourself** that **you** may know what is. . .Whatever **you** will open for **yourself**, **you** will open.* [Bolds ours]

Chapter Three

*Without going outside you may know the
whole world. Without looking through the
window you may know the ways of
heaven.*   —Lao Tzu

Spiritual Awareness

You've learned that the word spiritual originally meant awareness of your true nature 'in spirit.' We said earlier that this state of awareness requires a change of consciousness. That may sound difficult, but keep in mind that the Divine wants to be found and experienced, so this change is well within your reach. No methods, formulas, rituals or so-called 'spiritual' practices are required. Let's return to Rumi's eloquent description of the 'conversation' we were meant to enjoy:

> *Make everything in you an ear, each atom of your being, and you will hear at every moment what the Source is whispering to you, just to you and for you, without any*

need for my words or anyone else's. You are—we all are—the beloved of the Beloved, and in every moment, in every event of your life, the Beloved is whispering to you exactly what you need to hear and know. Who can ever explain this miracle? It simply is. Listen and you will discover it every passing moment. Listen, and your whole life will become a conversation in thought and act between you and Him, directly, wordlessly, now and always. It was to enjoy this conversation that you and I were created.

The shift in consciousness takes place when you're willing to stop letting your brain direct your thoughts and connect with the Divine via shared consciousness. That may sound odd, but scientists are discovering that the brain and the mind are two very different things. The brain is actually a receiving unit, retrieval system and data bank, much like a sophisticated computer program that manages a vast amount of data. Research is also demonstrating that the mind is a field that exists outside material reality. As you've probably already realized, the mind and shared consciousness are the same.

The brain is supposed to serve the mind, but it's also capable of shutting out the mind and running things on its own. When that happens, we become disconnected from our spiritual awareness. The brain takes in information through the senses and sorts it according to its own value system. Survival of the body is the brain's highest priority. When the brain is in charge, the choices it makes will serve the body and ignore the mind. When the mind is ignored, so is our connection with Ultimate Reality.

We can experience our connection with Divine consciousness when we let go of the brain's social conditioning, preconceived notions, attachments and aversions. Until we do that, the brain will insist on arguing with every thought that conflicts with its own beliefs. Once we've done that, we've put ourselves in a state of willingness and receptivity and can begin to hear what the Divine is telling us.

When you're spiritual, you're aware that you're alive 'in spirit' because you're connected with shared consciousness and experiencing it on a day-to-day basis. The writer of the *Mundaka Upanishad* summed up the experience of being 'in spirit:'

> *Self is everywhere, shining forth from all beings, vaster than the vast, subtler than the most subtle, unreachable, yet nearer than breath, than heartbeat. Ear cannot hear it nor tongue utter it; only in deep absorption can the mind, grown pure and silent, merge with the formless truth. He who finds it is free; he has found himself;*

he has solved the great riddle; his heart is forever at peace.

It's obvious from our brief examination of word origins that religious and spiritual once described very different ways to approach the Divine. Even now, you may have strong feelings concerning one approach or the other. But as we continue to explore the differences, you'll gain a deeper understanding of each approach and how they affect your happiness.

Part Two:
Religious

Chapter Four

Truth is a mirror in God's hand. It fell and broke. Everyone took a peice, looked at it, and thought they had the truth. —Rumi

What Religious Means

The word religion evolved from a variety of related words. The French *religare* meant "to bind fast, to restrain or tie back." This referred to an obligation or contract that bound humans to gods. This type of contractual arrangement is seen in the covenant between Jehovah and the Jewish people that was mediated by Moses when they accepted a code of laws symbolized by the Ten Commandments. For many Christians, baptism is considered a rite of admission that binds the baptismal candidate to the church.

The Latin word *religio* referred to restraints put on humans by supernatural beings. Religion is based on a hierarchy that places superhuman beings in a superior position over material beings who owe them worshipful obedience. Most religions also recognize evil supernatural beings that have been given power to torment humans. This hierarchy puts humans in a relatively powerless position that's equivalent to being restrained.

And the Latin *relegare* literally meant "read again," or the repetitious readings of texts that are considered holy. A feature that has always been prominent in religion is chanting, group reading, the repeating of creeds and prayers and singing from hymnals. The meanings of the words *religare, religio* and *relegare* were eventually combined to describe an organized body of believers that agree to:

■ bind themselves to certain supernatural powers, giving them exclusive devotion

■ conform to a particular set of doctrines, rules and moral values

■ adhere to a specific interpretation of text
 they consider holy

The current definition of the word religion remains very similar to the ancient origins of the word. We still generally think of a religious person as one who's affiliated with an organized group that's bound to a specific belief system. Many diverse groups may use the same holy book, but a religious person professes allegiance to the specific interpretation of that book that's endorsed by their church. It's said that there's somewhere between 30,000 to 40,000 Christian denominations that all accept the Bible as their sacred text, but disagree on the interpretation, doctrines, rules and values they each accept. Once again we're back to the problems innate to language. If all word meanings remained the same and everyone agreed to the same meanings, there would be no need for separate denominations that support their own interpretation of the same holy book.

Religion Evolves

Since we've seen that the 'spiritual' path is a do-it-yourself experience that has no structure, and religion is the embodiment of structure, let's look at how and why religious structure came about. The earliest religions evolved as a way to explain and deal with natural phenomenon. Fires, floods, earthquakes, tornadoes, hurricanes and volcanic eruptions appeared to be the work of superhuman beings who must be appeased. Ancient people depending on hunting, gathering or crops to sustain life on a day-to-day basis were extremely interested in doing everything possible to ensure their success. Eventually communities found it expedient to support someone who would take on the job of appeasing the gods on their behalf. This person, or group of people, divined what the gods wanted and conducted sacrifices, rituals and celebrations to curry the god's favor. As these observances became more elaborate and sophisticated, religious leaders kept their 'sacred knowledge' secret. As the gap between religious leaders and the common people widened, religious leaders gained authority, wealth and power.

The division between 'leaders' and 'followers' has remained a hallmark of nearly every religion. Today, leaders make up a clergy class, and followers are known as the laity class. We found it very interesting to discover that the original meaning of clergy signified an "office of dignity given to a person of learning" while the laity was considered "unlearned." This makes sense because holy books were rarely available to the masses until the printing press was invented and literacy spread. The clergy were among the few who were educated and had access to hand copied texts. The words clergy and laity also denoted the difference between a religious 'professional' and an 'amateur.'

Unlike sports, in religion few amateurs have the goal of turning professional. This is mainly because it's believed that the clergy have a special calling that the laity does not receive. This belief appears in many religions and fits with the idea that the laity class is made up of "unlearned amateurs." In the early Catholic Church, the clergy class believed the laity class was completely incapable of having a direct relationship with God or Christ. They saw themselves as mediators and guides who had the job of deciding what was right and wrong. In many cases, the laity still feels they have no need to understand religious matters since the clergy will take care of things for them.

Up until the last 200-300 years, religion and politics were allied in a symbiotic relationship that strengthened both groups. It was not uncommon for priests and kings to hold the same degree of power or for a king to be considered the head of the church. Religion was part of the cultural fabric of most societies, and it was as important to be an upstanding church member as it was to be a good citizen. Often they were considered the same thing. Attending and financially supporting the church was not a choice if you wanted to be an accepted part of the community. Lapses in belief and obedience often met with censure. Discipline could include penance, shunning, being barred from church sacraments and excommunication (expulsion).

During the last 50 years or so, the definition of a religious person still includes being affiliated with a specific belief system, but that affiliation can be quite loose. Currently, it's fairly common for church members to openly disagree with their church's belief system or live outside its moral code without discipline or censure. Many religious people also consider themselves 'lapsed.' In other words, they rarely attend religious services and may not support the church financially, but continue to feel some connection with it. Others may be regular participants, but are more interested in the social aspects of the church than the religious beliefs.

Most people who are active in a religion feel their lives are enriched by a sense of community, rich traditions, confirming rituals and uplifting emotion. Many enjoy the ceremony, music, art and architecture. Others appreciate the structure and rules that guides their day-to-day life. Some appreciate having a priest or minister available to answer questions, give guidance and preside over many of life's important events. Church members often feel that the size, scope and longevity of their religion confer a sense of 'rightness' and confidence that God approves of them. Certainly religion offers many benefits that may not be available to the more solitary spiritual seeker, but what is the cost of those benefits?

Chapter Five

No one saves us but ourselves. No one can and no one may. We ourselves must walk the path. —Buddha

The Master is Elevated

Most of the religions prominent today began with the teachings of a charismatic teacher/master/guru that appeared to be inspired. We would argue that many masters were indeed 'in spirit' when they delivered their message. They opened themselves to a higher level of awareness than most people ever experience, so they appeared to be extraordinary. Since their message came from higher consciousness, it sounded like it came from another world to those whose thinking was limited to the brain. Keep in mind that higher awareness is a state we can all access, and does not mean that the one who achieves it has any special powers. Regardless, the insights that come out of that state are remarkable and life-changing. Coming into contact with a spiritual master can have dramatic results, some positive, some negative. Let's look at what can happen.

A spiritual master knows that they have no unique abilities or special connection with the Divine. Above all else, they want their listeners to understand that they too can experience the same direct connection with the Divine the master has experienced. A master wants followers to use their message only as encouragement and a jumping off point for their own spiritual exploration, not as a guidebook. Unfortunately most people react to a spiritual master in a very different way.

Followers often see the master as unique or even superhuman. They mistakenly convince themselves that the master has a special connection with the Divine they could never have. Some followers may feel unable, or even uninterested, in reaching spiritual awareness, so this idea serves as an excuse. Others might be so enmeshed in life's problems; they need to see the master as a hero who will miraculously solve their problems for them. When any of these things happen, the master is robbed of her/his humanity. Instead of pursuing experiential knowing on their own, followers convince themselves that worship and obedience are the proper responses. This happens even when the master gives no instructions. The followers are so certain they must obey, they regularly make up their own instructions.

Raising the master to the point where they become impossible to imitate lets followers off the hook of self-responsibility. Worshipers expect their deified master to act as a mediator between them and the Divine. In return for this service, they believe they can offer the payment of worship and obedience. Unfortunately few worshipers ever wonder if this arrangement is desirable to their object of worship, or if it's actually working. Since a spiritual master wouldn't want, need or accept worship or obedience, this "exchange" amounts to wishful thinking on the part of the follower. And, since no one can experience the Divine for us, worshippers who want a mediator are cutting themselves out of the direct relationship with the Divine that could set them free. The only thing a master can do is show others that the door is open and demonstrate that each person must walk through on their own.

Jesus made the next two statements we'll be discussing for an extremely important reason.

You will know the truth, and the truth will set you free. (John 8:32)

Ask, and it will be given you; seek, and you will find; knock, and it will be opened

*to you. For everyone who asks receives,
and he who seeks finds, and to him who
knocks it will be opened.* (Matthew 7:-8)

It's commonly thought that Jesus was telling
his followers they could be set free by listening
to him, but when we look at his statement from
the standpoint of experiential knowing, it means
something quite different. He was telling his
followers that when they had a direct experience
of the Divine, they would see the universe in a
different way. They would 'know' the truth
through experience, and that truth would set
them free from the misperceptions that made
them miserable. As long as they looked at the
world through their senses and the brain's
perception, they would be stuck. When they
began thinking with shared, higher
consciousness, they would be free.

Jesus wasn't offering to do anything on anyone's
behalf; he was telling them they must 'know'

the truth for themselves, just as he had. As the poet John Keats noted, "Nothing ever becomes real till it is experienced. Even a proverb is no proverb to you till your life has illustrated it." And we all know that it's impossible for someone to experience for us. Alan Watts pointed out how differently information and experience operate when he said, "We can pool information about expereince, but never the expereinces themselves."

Jesus clearly told his followers what he had done, and that they all had the ability to do the same. Jesus didn't experience the Divine through anyone else, and he knew that he couldn't expereince the Divine *for* his followers. Therefore it was up to each of them, and each of us, to ask, seek and knock before the door can be opened and the answers discovered:

> **Ask**, *and it will be given you;* **seek**, *and you will find;* **knock**, *and it will be*

opened to you. For everyone who asks
receives, *and he who seeks* ***finds***, *and*
to him who knocks it will be ***opened***.

This text is often used to explain that we can expect God to give us help in trying circustances or material blessings when we ask for them, but when we look closer, we can see that Jesus was talking about a direct connection with the Divine. Jesus understood that a door exists between the brain and the mind that must be opened to access shared consciousness. Asking, seeking and knocking on the door all symbolize our willingness to let go of the brain's preconceived notions and open ourselves to the One Mind of shared consciousness. Regardless, we're the ones who have to do the asking, seeking and knocking since no one else can do it for us.

Let's read the words of the gnostic teacher Silvanus once more, but with a different emphasis:

> Bring in **your** guide and **your** teacher...Live according to **your** mind. . . Enlighten **your** mind. . .Light the lamp within **you**."

This verse leaves no room for second-hand information, but expects our personal experiences to change us. Of course there are people who are active in religion who seek out a first-hand connection with the Divine, but more often than not, religion encourages adherents to put worship and obedience first.

Followers who end up as worshipers usually believe their master is set apart in history. Worshippers have convinced themselves that no one came before, or will ever come again, who can compare to the master they follow. To support their claim, stories told about the master must become more and more grandiose. If you look at some of the earliest writings about Jesus (found in the sayings gospel known as Q), you'll see that early Christians thought of him as a wisdom teacher who was human in every respect. As you progress through Mark, Matthew, Luke and John, Jesus gradually changes. Early followers changed Jesus from an ordinary human to a 'special' human that God adopted as a son. The writer of the Bible gospel Luke claimed Jesus was a half man/half god (demi-god) who was begotten by Holy Spirit. Then some early Christians went a step further and claimed Jesus was a God in his own right who had come directly from heaven. Others said Jesus was actually the God of the Bible come to earth. Jesus was also made part of a 'Godhead' consisting of God, Jesus and Holy Spirit. Which was he? Does it matter?

If Jesus was a human wisdom teacher, he was telling you that you are just like him, and you can also experience the Divine for yourself. If he was adopted by God that means you have to be special or have a calling before you can experience the Divine. If Jesus was a supernatural being who came to earth, your only choice is to believe, obey and hope you are doing enough to please him. You may be interested to know that the question of Jesus' identity caused bitter, bloody battles to be fought within the Catholic Church for hundreds of years until the Roman Emperor Theodosius ended the fight by deciding in favor of the trinity doctrine and declaring Christianity the state religion of the Roman Empire. As an arm of the state, the church then committed itself to the extermination of anyone who disagreed with their picture of Jesus.

(The history of Jesus' transformation from human to God, and the changes that were made in early Christian writings to accommodate that transformation, are traced in detail in our book, *The Beginning of Fearlessness: Quantum Prodigal Son.*)

Whenever a master is elevated, the objective shifts from self-responsibility, personal 'knowing' and a direct experience of the Divine to worship, obedience and second-hand information about someone else's perception of the Divine. Which would you rather have?

The Message Becomes Sacred

When people begin to believe a master can never be equaled, it follows that they also believe the master's message will never be surpassed. By the time the message has wide distribution adherents are usually convinced it is God's direct message to the world. At that point, followers usually believe its integrity must be protected at all cost. However, when we read such a text, we need to think about how it came into existence.

Most religions teach that their holy book is based on eyewitness testimonials, but that's rarely the case. For example, Jesus' followers couldn't read or write, so they passed their stories orally. Since language, perception and memory are all unreliable, that leaves a very large margin for error. What if only 3-4 out of 100 eyewitnesses actually understood Jesus' message? And when those listeners passed on the message, what if only 5 of the 1,000 people who heard it understood what they had been told? It doesn't take long until the message bears little resemblance to the original. In Jesus' case, it wasn't until 25-75 years after his death that more educated converts, who spoke a different language, began writing down the stories they had been told. How much had the message changed during that time?

If it were possible to go back in time and see what a spiritual master actually did and said, it would probably bear little resemblance to the story that's told today. Even if we had a video of a master or a text written in their own hand, each follower still would come away with a different understanding because they hear the words from their own perspective. This is inevitable. Each of us has a different background, and our understanding is always filtered through our own personal experiences, education and social bias. Plus, we each have the brain to contend with, and the brain always opts for keeping the status quo. Anything that doesn't agree with the information it's already accumulated is rejected unless the brain believes it's necessary to sustain or better its life. We think absolute truth exists in our world, but perception makes objective reality impossible in the material universe.

Much as we might like to believe that we're accurate observers, our perception is extremely limited and untrustworthy. We can only take in a small percentage of the information that bombards us at any given moment. What we miss, the brain makes up, and it completes the story in a way that will synchronize with our past experiences and current beliefs. That's why 10 people can listen to one teacher and all come away with contradictory ideas. The One Mind is the seat of reality where truth can be found. There is only one way to access truth; bypass the brain, tune into the One Mind/shared consciousness and experience truth directly. Perception that results from the senses and the brain tells us what we *want* to know, vision that comes through *gnosis* shows us what we *need* to know.

We must also take into consideration the fact that sacred texts have been purposely altered on a regular basis. Everyone has an agenda, and no matter how pure that agenda is, it still colors everything we do and say. Some followers want to reinforce their personal views or disprove the views of their opponents. They may also dull or sharpen a master's message because they think it will attract more adherents. We have the luxury of printed material that remains constant over time, but up until a few hundred years ago sacred texts were copied over and over by hand. Many of these copied texts are riddled with errors, and some of those errors change the meaning of the message. Also, most sacred texts have been translated hundreds of times and suffered from the inability to express a thought accurately in another language. And as we said earlier, word meanings can change drastically over time and the original meaning can easily be lost or misunderstood.

When people become too deeply attached to either a master or the master's message, they mistakenly feel they must 'own' it. They feel certain that God has preserved their particular version, translation or interpretation and rejected everyone else's. They believe their understanding of the master's teaching is correct, and they must protect their interpretation from the perceptions of others.

They have no way to prove that they're correct, still, countless gallons of blood have been spilled defending the claim.

A spiritual message is valuable only as long as it frees us to explore and connect with the Divine directly. The moment a particular interpretation is considered inviolate, the message becomes static. At that point, the reader is limited to hearing a specific interpretation and obeying it. If their inner voice tells them something different, they're forced to reject it in favor of the text. As soon as a text is considered sacred or holy, the words have become more valuable than the spiritual experience that brought them into existence. The origins of the words 'holy' and 'sacred' are obscure, but they're generally believed to have come from the German *heilig* and the Latin *sanctus*. Both words signify something that must be preserved whole or intact, that cannot be transgressed or violated. Some religions take these meanings so seriously, they become literalists or fundamentalists.

For our purposes, we'll define literalism as the belief that God inspired a specific religious text, the text is unique, and it represents the only belief system that leads to salvation. On that basis, most of the world's religions can be considered literalist. Fundamentalists go even farther, taking each and every word in their sacred text at face value. Fundamentalists refuse to consider that words may have been mistranslated, purposely changed, had a different meaning when they were originally written or have a symbolic meaning. They cling to the text even when it's obviously illogical, irrelevant, outdated or unscientific. Fundamentalists often feel justified in going to almost any lengths to protect their text and spread its message.

Binding ourselves to a specific belief system robs us of the freedom of thinking for ourselves, making choices and trusting our own inner voice. Worse than that, it implies that we're incapable or unworthy of doing so. Clinging to a belief system allows someone else who claims to be more qualified, do our thinking for us. Letting someone else think for us may be easier, but we do it at the expense of sacrificing our personal power. Restricting ourselves to one thought system closes our mind to a multitude of possibilities and cuts us off from the direct experience of the Divine. It also creates the "my religion vs. the world" attitude that could potentially tear our world apart.

Chapter Six

Most people are other people. Their thoughts are someone else's opinions, their lives a mimicry, their passions a quotation. —Oscar Wilde

The Price of Structure

Once a spiritual master and their message are considered 'holy,' and a group of people have organized to protect and further that belief system, a clergy class and rules soon follow. Rules are necessary only when people believe they must preserve the sanctity of their religion and enforce the belief system. When we experience the Divine directly, no rules are needed because there is nothing to preserve or enforce. No one can argue with you over the rightness of your experience because it's yours alone. Since we're all different, we each experience the Divine in our own way. Those who have had that experience themselves realize this, and they have no need to argue with someone else's direct experience.

Most organizational structures in religion are based on the premise that humans are sinful, too weak and not intelligent enough to govern their own thoughts and actions. Rules are constructed to restrict the thoughts and control the behavior of believers so they won't fall into the hands of evil supernatural beings or be condemned by the God they worship. These rules must be explained and enforced, so a clergy class is formed to take care of these duties. Most church members would argue that rules are a necessary part of any organization. And they may also feel that the division between clergy and laity is essential since someone has to organize the group, care for their needs and dispense the message. Is this true?

The writers of the New Testament gospels claimed that Jesus treated his followers as if he was their leader and gave them instructions and rules they must follow if they were to gain salvation. However, in the gnostic *Gospel of Mary* Jesus told his followers not to "lay down any rules" or "make laws." The gnostic *Gospel of Thomas* reports that when Jesus was asked to rule on matters of the flesh he replied, "Do not tell lies and do not do what you hate." This admonition cannot be defined as a rule or law because it relies on personal assessment.

Since objective reality doesn't exist in the material world, no one can accurately assess whether someone else is lying or doing what they hate. Jesus' recommendation takes our thoughts and behavior from the religious arena and places it at the level of personal responsibility where it belongs. The Christian gnostic gospels are as old as the gospels found in the New Testament. Since it's impossible to prove which accounts are more accurate, it makes sense for thinking Christians to examine the gnostic gospels as well as the New Testament.

Although most religions claim that their rules and moral codes were decreed by God, spiritual masters understand that the only law that's necessary is the law of love. As Rumi said, "Divine laws are simpler than human ones—which is why it can take a lifetime to be able to understand them. Only love can understand them." Jesus also explained to his Jewish listeners that the entire set of religious laws that governed every part of their lives could be discarded if only they would practice the law of love.

No one can argue with the fact that rules and judgment go hand-in-hand. Without rules, no thought or action could be judged. Rules and judgment create a needless barrier of guilt and shame. Instead of helping people feel worthy of a direct connection with the Divine, judgment produces a feeling of worthlessness, defeat and fear. Rules and judgment are far more effective in controlling and subjugating people then they are in freeing them. Spiritual masters understand that our limited perception makes accurate judgment impossible. They refuse to judge others and refuse to accept the judgments others pass on them. Like Ultimate Reality, they "support all and choose all." (The gnostic *Gospel of Truth*)

Clergy

We've been taught to think of a master as a leader, but is that their function? What does the term 'master' really mean? If we look at the word from a spiritual sense, a master is a person who has mastered their own misperceptions. They now think from the One Mind of higher consciousness, not the brain. They want to help set others free, not control or direct them. In the gnostic *Gospel of Thomas* Jesus said:

> *I am not your master. . .He who will drink from my mouth will become as I am; I myself shall become he, and the things that are hidden will be revealed to him.*

Jesus understood that when his followers had their own direct experience of the Divine, they would 'know' exactly what he knew and they would understand the oneness of all things. He could serve as an example and an encouragement, but only the experience itself could wake them up to that oneness. In the gnostic *Testimony of Truth,* Jesus said that every seeker must become the "disciple of his [own] mind." When each person experiences the Divine for themselves, the concept of mastery or leadership over another becomes ridiculous.

Any group usually requires at least a minimal amount of organization to function, but in the case of religion, rules and the division between clergy and laity have also brought immense power and wealth to church hierarchies. Although power and wealth can obviously be used for good, what is this arrangement costing the laity? Certainly the financial drain that supporting the clergy and the cost of building and maintaining church buildings can be a heavy burden. But the real problem occurs when church members are convinced that their relationship with God, or their salvation, is tied to the financial support they give the church. In contrast, the direct experience of the Divine is absolutely free and accessible to anyone at any time or place.

No matter how sincere and helpful some members of the clergy may be, this hierarchy creates a barrier between the laity and their own experience of the Divine. The positive emotions that can be felt during a moving sermon, prayer or religious celebration cannot begin to compare with the value of higher awareness and the direct experience of the Divine. Once again, let's consider what Rumi had to say about a direct connection with the Divine:

> *The Beloved is whispering to you exactly what you need to hear and know. Who can ever explain this miracle? It simply is. Listen and you will discover it every passing moment. Listen, and your whole life will become a conversation in thought and act between you and Him, directly, wordlessly, now and always. It was to enjoy this conversation that you and I were created.*

Are you willing to give up this conversation and the direction you can receive from the Divine that's meant especially for you? No other person, no matter how learned or wise they appear to be, can know exactly what you need or offer you such tailor-made support.

The division between the laity and clergy also gives the very false impression that only a few people with special attributes or a 'calling' are meant to experience the Divine. But the gnostic *Gospel of Truth* explains:

> *The Father's Word goes out in the All as the fruition of his heart and expression of his will. It supports all and chooses all.*

Since everything is the Divine, how could one person be considered special and another not? That would be the same as saying some parts of God are special and other parts aren't. Everyone is called and chosen, the problem is that most of us have been taught not to listen for the call or feel worthy of it if we do hear it. But how could you not be worthy to experience the Divine since you *are* divine?

Part Three:
Doing or Being

Chapter Seven

When you reach the end of what you know, you will be at the beginning of what you should sense. —Khalil Gibran

Will You Do, Or Be?

The most decisive difference between religion and spirituality is doing vs. being. Doing centers on the body, being focuses on the higher awareness of the mind. When we're 'doing' the brain is in charge, and the mind is rarely heard. Although everyone has the capacity to think with the mind and experience the Divine directly, it becomes far more difficult when the body and brain are engaged in 'doing.'

Doing

It may surprise you to realize just how much religion focuses on the body. Of course the body actively attends and participates in church services, celebrations, sacraments, social groups and religious classes. Many religions teach that faith must be accompanied by works, so the body participates in service to the church and the community. Religious services are designed to engage the body's emotions. The feelings elicited can run the gamut from love and joy to fear and shame, but all emotion keeps the body involved. Some religions encourage their adherents to go farther than just feelings and express their emotions by shouting, dancing, clapping, speaking in tongues, etc., which all involve the body.

Churches themselves and the services held within them appeal to the body's senses. During church services and celebrations the ears hear preaching, singing, instrumental music, chanting and readings. The mouth tastes sacramental offerings like bread and wine, and foods related to celebrations. The eyes see impressive architecture and inspiring art. The nose smells incense and flowers. The body may go through several changes in posture and feel many textures during the course of a church service. The brain is engaged at the intellectual level while taking in information and sorting through it during sermons and classes. The brain and body work together as physical rituals are preformed, sacred texts are read and prayers are said or repeated.

Most religious rules involve controlling the emotions and actions of the body and the thoughts of the brain. Confession centers on the ways the body has fallen short of expected behavior. Acts of contrition and penance usually require the body's involvement as well. At times, adherents are expected to control or physically punish the body by fasting, crawling, sitting for extended periods of time, carrying heavy objects or even purposely injuring themselves.

Religious rules also give the strong impression that God is extremely interested in what bodies do. Many religions focus so strongly on rules that control the body; adherents believe that their everlasting life depends strictly on their ability to control the body. This thought can be very frustrating since they're also told the body is sinful and incapable of perfect behavior. A well-known saying, "idle hands are the devil's workshop," highlights the belief that keeping the body busy is an important part of religion. Many religious people never even contemplate having a direct experience of the Divine because they're so focused on 'doing' and controlling the body.

Being

Spirituality turns our focus away from the body and directs it toward our connection with the One Mind of shared, higher consciousness. The actions of the body have nothing to do with awareness. The body does not have to be in a certain position to experience the Divine, it can happen any time and in any place. Some teachers claim that meditation is essential to reach higher states of awareness, but that brings the focus back to controlling the body. Yoga works the same way; it's a method of controlling the body that's supposed to lead to the ability to focus the mind and reach higher states of awareness. There's certainly nothing wrong with meditating or practicing yoga *if it works for you,* but a recent study has shown that a whopping 54% of people who meditate actually feel more anxious from the practice. Just remember that no methods or practices are necessary to make a direct connection with the Divine. If not, how is higher awareness reached?

Spiritual masters have often mentioned three fundamental qualities common to successful spiritual seekers, but none of these basic characteristics requires anything other than a particular mindset and a willingness to have your misperceptions corrected. These qualities are free and available to everyone, no matter what our circumstances might be. The first is a 'pure heart,' but that doesn't mean we need to 'clean up our act.' A pure heart concerns motive. Many seek a relationship with God because they want something or because they're afraid not to. A pure heart symbolizes our desire to know the Divine for the sheer joy and freedom that's inherent in the relationship. Jesus mentioned the next quality during his Sermon on the Mount when he said "blessed are the poor in spirit."

What does 'poor in spirit' actually mean? Since we're often confronted by the image of the ascetic spiritual master who renounces all material comforts and desires, it's easy to confuse literal poverty with a poor spirit. But poverty is a detriment and distraction, not an asset, to spiritual awareness. Having material comforts isn't a spiritual problem in itself; the only issue is how much we allow them to distract us from something that's far more valuable. Being poor in spirit means that although we've experienced what the world has to offer, we still feel an emptiness that can't be filled by anything outside us. This does not mean that we find no happiness in life, give up material comforts or stop pursuing experiences that bring us pleasure. It only means that we no longer see things, experiences or relationships as an end in themselves. We know the world can make us rich, but it cannot enrich us.

The third quality has been called 'empty hands' or 'beginner's mind.' If we're trying to corroborate our preexisting beliefs, our hands are already full. Full hands cannot hold anything new. When we cling to preconceived notions, our brains work overtime to prove that we're right. They focus on anything that supports our belief system and filters out everything else. The spiritual seeker lets go of all preconceived notions, personal preferences and attachments or aversions to particular outcomes and is willing to receive something new. Experts cling to the information they've already collected and argue in favor of it, but a beginner's mind is open to whatever possibilities appear. The key to having a direct experience of the Divine and connecting with shared consciousness is willingness, the willingness to listen and be amazed.

Thc brain is petty and concentrates on its own well-being. Higher, shared consciousness sees the complete picture. It is well aware of the oneness of all things and the love that unites everything in existence. When we experience the Divine firsthand, we no longer need rules that focus on the body. We understand that the Divine doesn't make rules that restrict and control the body or the emotions, and we won't be judged on the basis of rules that human brains have concocted. Like Jesus, we understand that we can trust the law of love to direct our behavior.

Spirituality is not a group activity. Experiencing the Divine is personal, and requires us to make the effort to let go of our preconceived notions so we can hear what the One Mind is telling us. That's not to say that the spiritual person needs to be an isolationist. Spiritual masters live a balanced life of introspection and social interaction. Unfortunately many people have associated spiritual mastery with asceticism and isolation; a direct connection with the Divine speaks more to abundance and interaction than scarcity and isolation.

Most religious people feel that it's their duty to convince others of the 'rightness' of their message. A spiritual person sees no reason to proselytize. They know that words can't describe their experience, and it wouldn't be helpful anyway because each person experiences the Divine in the way that's best suited to them. A spiritual person may be very private, or they may wish to share the fact that this state of awareness is within the reach of anyone who wants to experience it. They keep in mind the concept expressed by Albert Einstein when he said, "Setting an example is not the main means of influencing others, it's the only means." Regardless, they know that spiritual awareness is based on free will and conversion is impossible.

When we connect with the mind, our life becomes a conversation with the Divine. The brain believes that it's able to make informed decisions, but the mind actually knows what's best for us in every circumstance. As we learn to hear the mind and trust it, we lose our fear and live the life of fearlessness, peace and joy we all deserve. A direct connection to the Divine allows us to see that there is no distance between us and the Divine. We are made of the very 'stuff of God' and have no need to be 'saved' from the imagined sinfulness imposed by religion. We need no rules or moral codes to live by as we apply the law of love in each circumstance. We understand that obedience, worship and sacrifice are impossible and ridiculous. As we see the oneness of all things in existence, we realize we have no need for intermediaries or saviors. As Jesus said, "You will know the truth, and the truth will set you free."

Can the way you approach God affect your happiness? Does it really matter whether you're religious or spiritual? Is there any real difference between the two? We can only answer yes, yes, and yes. The meaning of the word spiritual has changed so drastically, the direct approach to God has been lost. We've forgotten that we each have the ability to have a direct experience of the Divine. We've forgotten how to trust ourselves, listen to our inner voice, and connect with everything in existence .

When we remember, we lose our fears and experience life in an entirely new way. Rumi explained that when we believe that we are this brain/body, we're like a priceless sword encrusted with jewels that's being used in a butcher shop to cut up rancid meat or a golden bowl that's being used to cook turnips. We insist that we're putting these items to good use, but they were not meant for these lowly purposes.

Instead, Rumi encourages you to experience the Divine for yourself and know who you really are:

> *You were born of the rays of God's majesty. . .how long will you suffer at the hands of non-existent things? You are a ruby in the heart of granite, how long will you try to deceive us? We can see the truth*

in your eyes, so come, come, return to the root of the root of you own Self.

Thank you for taking the time to read:

Religious or Spiritual: How the Difference Can Affect Your Happiness.

We realize this discussion has probably brought many questions to mind.

As we look at the miserable condition of the world, it seems impossible for a God of love to exist. The "question of evil," is answered in our book, **The Beginning of Fearlessness: Quantum Prodigal Son**. The book contains a verse-by-verse discussion of Jesus' parable of the prodigal son as seen through the lens of quantum physics, the gnostic gospels and the perennial philosophy. Understand Jesus' teachings in an exciting, and liberating new way.

If you would like to learn more about the gnostic gospels and Jesus' gnostic teachings, you might also enjoy **The Gospel of Thomas: Where Science Meets Spirituality.** Both books by

Lee and Steven Hager are available in ebook and print formats through most online retailers and at **The Beginning of Fearlessness/ Oroborus Books website and blog**:

http://www.thebeginningoffearlessness.com

The Divine manifestation is ubiquitous, only our eyes are not open to it
—Joseph Campbell

The end of all our exploring will be to arrive where we started and know the place for the first time. —T. S. Eliot

There is nothing outside yourself, look within. Everything you want is there.
—Rumi

Index

Religious or Spiritual

C

D

Religious or Spiritual

goddesses 25
Godhead 73
gods 25
Gospel of Mary, The 87
Gospel of Thomas, The 87, 90
Gospel of Truth, The 89, 93
group reading 56
guilt 88
guru 65

H

Hafiz 12
heaven 23
heilig 80
hell 23
hierarchy 55
higher, shared consciousness 37, 38
holy 57, 80, 85
holy book 75
humans as weak, sinful 86

I

ignorance 25
in spirit 37, 65
inanimate 20, 24
information 70, 75
intermediaries 107
interpretation 57

J

Jehovah 55
Jesus 68, 70
Jesus, as demigod 73
Jesus, as gnostic 41
Jesus, as God 73
Jesus, as human 73
Jesus, as leader 86

N

O

P

Religious or Spiritual

T

www.ingramcontent.com/pod-product-compliance
Lightning Source LLC
Chambersburg PA
CBHW020550030426
42337CB00013B/1031